SCHIRMER'S LIBRARY
OF MUSICAL CLASSICS

Vol. 33

FRÉDÉRIC CHOPIN

ETUDES

For the Piano

Revised and Fingered by

ARTHUR FRIEDHEIM

With a General Prefatory Note by

JAMES HUNEKER

and Introductory Remarks by

ARTHUR FRIEDHEIM

G. SCHIRMER, *Inc.*

DISTRIBUTED BY

Hal•Leonard®
CORPORATION
7777 W. BLUEMOUND RD. P.O. BOX 13819 MILWAUKEE, WI 53213

INTRODUCTORY

In every age there have been individuals who disputed the value of all tradition—if they did not roundly deny it. Now, hardly one case in a thousand is better adapted to lend countenance to such views, than the Chopin Edition of C. Mikuli. After the very rational, quietly objective Preface one would expect a trustworthy, well-informed guide through blest and unblest realms of enchantment; instead of which one usually finds himself confronted, so to speak, by a hedge of stubborn, thorny fingerings and shapelessly twisted, truncated expression- and tempo-marks, behind which a naughty rogue seems to be calling out mockingly at the trustful beginner: "Come along, keep on trying! you'll never get through!" At intervals may be found empty expanses where liberty reigns untrammeled, for nothing (aside from the bare framework of notes) is to be seen except a few wandering, scattered pedal-marks. Should the metronomic signpost happen to bear a number less than 20 degrees higher or lower than it ought to be, one is agreeably surprised. And the crowning joke is, that all this is supposed to be by the composer himself. Only one who feels impelled to follow up this "legitimate" apostle of Chopin measure by measure, is in a position thoroughly to appreciate all that has been achieved here on the basis of a most intimate misunderstanding of the instrument. However, the piano-playing world passed sentence on it long ago, so no further words are necessary.

None the less, any one who rejects tradition sets himself in opposition to the facts, as is evidenced by the history of the arts. Let us beware of taking the shadow for the substance.

With the present edition an attempt has even been made to establish a tradition at second-hand. True, the man from whom this tradition is derived was not merely by far the most renowned pianist of the last century, itself most productive of virtuosi (not to mention pioneer composers of the first rank), but also enjoyed, while a youth of nearly the same age as Chopin, such intimate intellectual intercourse with him that in Paris, in the early 'thirties, they were called the Dioscuri. The Études of Op. 10 are dedicated to Liszt, and the two friends discussed every detail most thoroughly before surrendering the booklet to the printer, as Liszt frequently related. Thus it is only natural that Liszt should have been the first to introduce Chopin's name to the European public on his concert-tours. And twenty years later he published a book which can never be surpassed, because

only a Liszt could write in such a manner about a Chopin. All who ever heard Liszt are agreed that he, after his so-called "best years," was the most objective piano-player that can be imagined, inasmuch as his entire individuality was merged in that of the composer whom he was interpreting —hence the convincing effect. Until the very end (in 1886) his intellectual vigor was astounding; and, although towards 1883 his sovereign mastery of technique began to abate, there were days when the old magic asserted itself in undiminished power, and the burden of age seemed to be thrown off. Now, when one has heard, let me say, the majority of these Études played repeatedly by Liszt; when, moreover, he has heard in hundreds of lessons and on other occasions pretty much everything that Liszt had to set forth concerning them; such a person must certainly be endowed with a remarkably treacherous memory if, after all this, he were not well posted. Here the objection will be raised, that as early as the 'fifties two Chopin editions had already emanated from Liszt's entourage, one of which was bad, and the other not good. Now then, the following explanation may sound jocular, but is meant quite seriously. At that time these young men were so fully under the obsession of the tendency then known as the "music of the future," that their minds were hardly accessible to anything else. Later, as their horizon broadened, they went their own way and achieved great things. Another striking example of this state of mind is found in Bülow's celebrated Beethoven edition, which, despite its many good points, in the main betrays to the initiated how little he had learned, at the time, from Liszt. Matters were different with young Anton Rubinstein, who might often have been seen at that period as a guest in Weimar. He had never been directly a pupil of Liszt's; at first, circumstances were to blame; but in Weimar he was already a finished artist, whereas others of the same age were still occupied in scaling the height of Parnassus. Rubinstein gave little heed to the music of the future as he went his way; on the other hand, he greedily absorbed from Liszt everything that suited his temperament. And while he approached Liszt more nearly than any of the others, he came nearest to him in his interpretation of Chopin's compositions.

Even as a boy, I was quite familiar with these twenty-seven Études; therefore, when I heard eight of them played in Petrograd by Rubinstein on an evening in 1873, the impression was all the stronger. Naturally, I missed no opportunity of hearkening to these revelations, and the years next ensuing afforded not a few. But when, after this, I came to Liszt, I soon became aware that I had now reached the true source of the Rubinstein revelation—without, of course, in the least belittling the value and greatness of the latter.

Now, while Liszt's career as a virtuoso was comparatively short, and much of his teaching fell, even with his best pupils, on barren ground, as the above-noted celebrated examples show, Rubinstein exercised a truly enormous pedagogical influence throughout his forty-year course as a concert-pianist. More especially during the last twenty years of his life, students and teachers everywhere stormed the concert-halls, no matter whether they had to pay high for their tickets or were granted free admission through Rubinstein's munificence. This influence makes itself felt down to the present day; for the youngest among our prominent pianists differ, on the whole, but little one from the other as regards conception. Be it understood, that this refers to Chopin exclusively. To a certain extent, therefore, a tradition actually exists—is alive; but as no one has hitherto thought to set it down on paper in a form as uncorrupt as possible, it was time that this should be done by one who is justified, by his own past experience, in giving his opinion in the matter.

Concerning the details of the present edition, the following observations are to be made.

First, with regard to the fingering. There is no infallible, universal fingering, because, on account of variability in the shape of the hand, none such can be formulated. But there is such a thing as a normal, average fingering which fits the majority of cases, and this principle we have adhered to; besides, the easiest fingering has always been adopted, as will soon be discovered even in those passages where, at first glance, it does not seem to be the case; even so, the pieces will generally be quite difficult enough. But any one who, for example, in a stretch can use the third finger to better advantage than the fourth, or *vice versa*, or who can take wide leaps with greater confidence by employing the thumb, etc., etc., should fall back on his or her own judgment. Contrariwise, the amateur—whose importance must not be underestimated, as he is the basic material of our audiences—is warned, in his own interest, not simply to ignore the given fingerings and allow Nature to take her course unheeding. Many an amateur, who is sufficiently musical and also has command of a fair technique, finds himself unable to master a piece otherwise seemingly within his powers, without realizing that his failure is caused by a fingering which, from the first measure, takes no account of what follows.

Similar caution, though in a quite different sense and with corresponding limitations, is applicable with respect to the pedalling. Whoever has attained to the point of mastering these Études both intellectually and technically will now and again hold the pedal down a trifle longer, or release it sooner, according to strength of finger, vigor of touch, and so forth; neither will he use the pedal in a room as he does in a large hall. At such a stage, one's own judgment and experience are the best teachers.

The metronomic markings are meant merely as aids, for the avoidance of serious misconceptions.

The matter of prime importance, however, in an edition founded on tradition, is the marks of interpretation; and in this regard the present edition varies in no small degree from all preceding ones. To begin with, the long slurs have been omitted, being replaced wherever necessary by the reiterated indication "legato"; the slurs, on the other hand, serve to set off the several periods and sections one from the other; that is, they apply to the phrasing. Furthermore, the obsolete sign *sf* is mostly dropped, because it tempts to an involuntary overexertion of force, and is replaced by the more modern $>$. Besides, all those arbitrary dynamic marks are omitted which are not found in the old editions. Instead, for the sake of precision and distinctness, various new markings have been inserted. For instance, Liszt often used to observe, "In order to produce an intensification, one should first diminish in force"; nevertheless, this elementary principle has never, in all the literature of the pianoforte, been carried out strictly enough—not even by him who spoke these words. And so, even if this edition itself cannot be wholly absolved of arbitrary traits, may the shade of Chopin approve my course in consideration of the purpose. For it has been my honest endeavor throughout, putting aside every personal suggestion from within or from without, to reproduce as nearly as might be a faithful image in notes of what I heard, three and four decades ago, in Petrograd, Weimar, and Rome.

New York, 1916. ARTHUR FRIEDHEIM

NOTES

TO ÉTUDE No. 1

Although in transparency of construction the most étude-like of Chopin's Études, this "runaway chorale" (as somebody once jestingly called it) rests on a harmonic foundation of fine music, beautiful in its simplicity. Its contours are indicated by the accents, which must, therefore, be strictly observed; they are omitted in only a few measures (42, 43 and 44), where the chord-figure emerges from the regular pattern and assumes a melodious guise on the third and fourth quarters. The historical significance of the Étude is found in the fact that here, for the first time, the octave-stretch is exceeded throughout; since then, it has hardly been surpassed in difficulty in this respect.

TO ÉTUDE No. 2

This Étude presents one of the masterkeys of technique, for it aims at equalizing the development of the third, fourth and fifth fingers of the right hand as regards their strength, flexibility and independence. The Mikuli fingering carries out this principle from beginning to end without the least concession to the power of endurance; consequently it may be used for practice by those who are confident that their muscles possess the needful powers of resistance without fear of harmful results. The fingering given here, on the contrary, is founded in the main on ease of execution; so wherever it is possible the fingers in question are allowed a respite, however short, and in wide stretches the passing over or under of the third finger is avoided. Only he who (as Anton Rubinstein admits having done in his youth) has spent years upon it, knows how difficult it is to attain the desired effect in playing this gloomy little mood-picture with the conciliatory closing chord.

TO ÉTUDE No. 3

One sometimes hears the wondering inquiry, What is the use of pieces in slow, sustained tempo as Études? The answer is, They are Studies in Touch. This Étude belongs to that class; for the double-notes in the subordinate section can scarcely be considered as a technical problem. The *cantilena*, with its dainty shading, should stand out plainly from the accompaniment; the gently pulsing accent on each eighth in the left hand throughout the first fifteen measures, and at the repetition of the principal theme, must be carefully observed. In the secondary theme, in the four measures of chromatic passages in diminished fifths and augmented fourths, the fingering for thirds is given for both hands; please refer to the remarks on this head appended to Étude No. 23.

TO ÉTUDE No. 4

For a long time this Étude was held to be the *non plus ultra* in finger-technique; and it is a fact that neither Chopin himself, nor any one after him, has essentially surpassed what is required here; more particularly in view of the often extremely crowded position and other inconveniences in the passage-work. Some few fingerings may appear strange at first glance; but not to those who are familiar with Étude No. 2. In certain places the accents serve to throw the harmonic framework into relief, as may be seen without special indications, and then they must be the more strongly emphasized. Neither can these accents be made too pointed in the right hand, eight measures before the close, on each final sixteenth in the quarter (and through the following three measures, as marked), otherwise the outline will be blurred and the proper ending of the piece robbed of its effect. The last four measures merely represent the dying-away of the closing chord.

TO ÉTUDE No. 5

A genuine Chopinesque stroke of genius is this "Étude on the Black Keys" (the designation halts, for it applies only to the right hand; but that is no fault of the composer's, because, as we know, he did not bestow any such titles on his works). Here Chopin (tentatively, as it were) for the first time employs a method which he developed on a very broad scale and with most purposeful effect in later Études; the melodic and thematic material is entrusted to the left hand, while the right carries on the given étude-figure in the shape of a sparkling commentary upon it, predominating only at occasional moments. Hence, the right hand is never to be subordinated in this Étude, whereas, in the left hand, the occasional answering part should be very discreetly brought out by means of slurs and accents. In this case the "Étude," on the whole, still keeps the upper hand. Against one vice of style the player is earnestly warned; in concerts nowadays one hears, now and again, the final octave-passage taken in the higher octave. Through the slight prolongation this finale takes on a somewhat cyclopean effect quite disproportionate to the entire piece foregoing. There are plenty of works—even some of Chopin's—where the telling effect of bravura octaves may be added—in the right place.

TO ÉTUDE No. 6

Here we are confronted by another "Study in Touch," of a character still more pronounced than No. 3; for while in this latter there are some few double-notes that not everybody can play at first sight, the figure in sixteenth-notes which is continued throughout this Étude can be called difficult solely as regards the mode of tone-production. Although one can hardly speak of polyphony, in the proper sense, nevertheless each part demands special consideration, even where they all meet in chord-like form. And one has to be all the more careful in this matter, because our only means of prolonging the tones, the pedal, can be used but little, on account of the sixteenth-figuration, and mostly on weak beats. Concerning the conception of the piece, one cannot go astray; it speaks too plain a language for that.

TO ÉTUDE No. 7

In the technical figure given to the right hand, on which this Étude is built up, the higher part should be played *legato* throughout, and the lower *staccato*. Therefore, in the higher part, every detached grouping of 2, 4, or more sixteenths, and any interruption where a tone happens to be repeated, must be avoided; whereas, in the lower part, nothing should be bound. Do not think that the rapid tempo renders such nicety superfluous; for even if very few auditors would notice such lapses from correctness in detail, the general effect intended by the composer would be impaired. The melody lies in the higher tones of the *legato* part, and therefore always falls on weak beats; consequently, such accents as occur must be emphasized as here marked, for an emphasis on strong beats is altogether senseless. Aside from the indicated accents, the left hand is nowhere to be made prominent, with one exception (through the four measures after the organ-point on G).

TO ÉTUDE No. 8

In the Note to No. 5 we already alluded to the mannerism (in the best sense) peculiar to Chopin of employing the "étude" in the right hand merely as an ornamental trimming, as it were, to the musical thought. In the present Étude it is strongly in evidence, the left hand taking the lead for the most part. The figuration in sixteenth-notes comes to the fore only occasionally and briefly, for the facilitation of transitions; otherwise the melodico-thematic thread is spun on uninterruptedly, and can readily be followed with the aid of the given slurs, accents, etc., while to the pedal is often entrusted the most important part in the prolongation of the emphasized notes, more especially in the right hand. Play the piece briskly and buoyantly. The four closing chords should be arpeggio'd note after note from the lowest in the left hand to the highest in the right. The classic arpeggio, in which the two hands start together, is nowhere to be employed in Chopin.

TO ÉTUDE No. 9

The musical content of this piece is of so pronounced a character, that when Chopin's Études for the left hand are enumerated among musicians, this one is either not mentioned at all, or named at the end with a smile. For it ought rather to be classed with the Studies in Touch, among which it ranks with the foremost in difficulty. Its ireful pathos and harsh contrasts show a remarkable spiritual kinship with Liszt. Misled thereby, Lina Ramann (Liszt's first biographer) asserts that the piece was written under Liszt's influence—without considering that it was written before they knew each other. Chopin assuredly assimilated the most various elements, otherwise his development could not have been what it was; but whatever the product which resulted therefrom, it always bears a stamp so sharply individual that one can never speak of the influence of this or that composer. In any event, spiritual kinship of this type is by no means a rarity in art.

TO ÉTUDE No. 10

This is, first and foremost, a rhythmical study; a fact which requires no special demonstration. It is equally evident that this Étude is also "profitable" in other ways. Its fundamental mood is radiant serenity; despite all its rhythmical vacillations and extreme mobility it should flow onward smoothly and evenly as though penetrated by the breath of springtide. The accents, even when some few chord-cloudlets momentarily darken the sunny landscape, must never become dramatic. In the last measure but one, the first eighth in the third quarter is to be sustained like a half-note. For this Mikuli provides no fingering at all, doubtless the editor's most convenient expedient. The fingering added here will almost invariably fail to work on first trial; but it will soon become apparent that the free entrance of the fifth finger on A♭ operates far more surely than the change from thumb to fifth finger, and for these reasons: you avoid striking the note again, which is apt to happen in the other case, and the next third can be taken much more easily. The point is important. A mistake in such an ending spoils the whole piece.

TO ÉTUDE No. 11

Hans von Bülow makes, in his edition, the incomprehensible mistake of expressly requiring the classic arpeggio here. So hardly any one has paid any attention to this direction; still, we shall emphatically repeat what was said in the Note to No. 8, that in all Chopin's compositions the arpeggios are to be played note after note from the lowest in the left hand to the highest in the right. In this Étude, everything without exception is to be arpeggio'd all the way through, including the two chord-appoggiaturas which lead over to the closing notes; this last would be sufficiently evident merely from the finishing touch in the left hand. The chief technical aim is found in the wide stretches; concurrently, the piece belongs among the Studies in Touch, as the melody does not lie in the highest part alone, but must occasionally be distinctly brought out in other parts. For instance, it is usually overlooked that, in measures 5 and 4 from the end, the melodico-thematic thread is taken over by the lower left-hand part, the contrasting higher right-hand part being merely cadential. Just here the following refinement should be noticed; between the above-mentioned measures the melody takes an upward turn, but in the next two it makes a downward, closing move. What comes after this, is a short Coda.

TO ÉTUDE No. 12

In the musical world an undeniable predilection for program-music is most naïvely manifested by the impulse to furnish titles for compositions which the Masters had left without such. To be sure, the selected titles are generally more or less irrelevant, as in the present case; for even if no one ever thought of calling the piece "Calm at Sea," a Revolution would certainly have taken on a more intensive form in Chopin's imagination. No. 23 is more like a "Revolution." The principal aim of this Study for the Left Hand is to teach the student to economize his strength. The player who husbands it for the climaxes, and carefully observes (simply from a technical standpoint) the accents and the numerous *crescendos* and *decrescendos,* will discover that the piece by no means demands such enormous powers of endurance as would appear needful at first glance. Beware of hurrying in the two passages where the octaves in the right hand momentarily coincide with the left hand in sixteenth-notes (repetition of the principal theme). Take the four closing chords strictly in time.

TO ÉTUDE No. 13

Although it was remarked, in connection with the preceding Étude, that arbitrarily selected titles are usually irrelevant and thus, at best, superfluous, this so-called "Harp-Study" forms an exception; for this by-name is directly misleading, for the reason, at the very least, that it raises a secondary matter to first importance. Chopin made his intention absolutely plain by having the first note of each group of sixteenths in the right hand engraved in larger type. The student will, therefore, do well to imagine the melody contained in these notes carried by an idealized wind-instrument, considering all else as accompaniment— in fact, as a piano-accompaniment; he had better keep the harp quite out of it. Any one who has heard this piece played by the finest of harpists, knows how beautifully it can be made to sound on the piano. The bass tones (also marked by larger type), all the incidental inner parts, and the after-striking octaves in the right hand shortly before the close, should be very discreetly emphasized. Avoid, wherever you can, the leap from the last sixteenth of the group to the next melody-note; then you will not only maintain the required *legato*, but also gain in confidence of attack.

TO ÉTUDE No. 14

Extreme smoothness and evenness are requisite in this Étude. In the transitions at the repetition and reëntrance of the principal theme it is, however, permissible to slow down the tempo imperceptibly. On the other hand, the *ritardando* indicated shortly before the close, and at the very close, must be most decidedly marked. The very last eighth-note group with the appoggiaturas is to be played as a quintuplet. In the *pianissimos* one may venture to the extreme; but the sole *forte* which occurs must sound rather subdued, and the various *crescendos* and *decrescendos* must be confined within the narrowest limits. The pedal-markings here are calculated in the main for small hands. Liszt employed the pedal far less—only for binding, in fact, or for mysteriously veiling some few short strains. But, from the very beginning, he did hold down each bass note in hand until the next change, as Klindworth indicates. The effect was admirable, and Chopin himself unquestionably performed the piece in a similar manner. But, whatever may have induced his choice of notation, there it stands as he set it down; and the editor's feeling of reverence revolts at the idea of altering essential note-values even suggestively throughout the piece. Hence, the "tradition" in its principal aspects is contained in the above observations.

TO ÉTUDE No. 15

By shifting the accents, this Étude becomes a Study in Rhythm; and by greatly varying the accentuation it is transformed into an extremely subtle Study in Touch. Towards the end the accents may occasionally sound pert and pointed, but never harsh; so take care to bring out a full, mellow tone. Do not excessively prolong the two *ritenutos* before the *forte* entries in B major and F major; play the closing measures, and also the final chords, strictly in time.

TO ÉTUDE No. 16

However masterly the pianoforte-style of this Étude may be—a matter of course with Chopin— the violin, with its manifold bowings and other effects, touched his fancy for the nonce. One thinks involuntarily of Paganini and his diabolical tricks of artistry; the right hand plays a mournful, agitated air, with a demoniacally seconding and contrasting left-hand part in burlesque *pizzicato*. Very special attention must be paid to the pedalling; every rest has meaning, and therefore should not be covered up or suppressed. Bring out the *crescendos* and *diminuendos* sharply, and give every contrast strong emphasis. In the fourth measure from the end the wild phantoms are laid; it is like awakening from a dream; therefore, on the last two quarters, both the *crescendo* and the pace must be suddenly restrained to the utmost, and the three *Lento* measures played with great deliberation, subsiding from *f* down to *pp*. This is another of the closes "where everything counts."

TO ÉTUDE No. 17

Once again a Study in Touch. The mood is not easily caught, for here one should "smile amid tears." First of all, therefore, aim for absolute correctness and for lightness; the rest will be added unto you according as essentials are present or absent. Furthermore, be particularly careful that the melodic flow is nowhere interrupted; slurs, accents, etc., indicate the course in a way scarcely to be misunderstood. Up to the last seventeen measures everything without exception is to be kept soft and subdued; then there comes an abrupt change. The four *piano* measures just before the close should be played in strict time and without expression, but the three preceding measures, as well as the thirteen measures succeeding, must be "declaimed" with the greatest energy. Do not hurry the eighth-note quintuplet in the last measure but one; it reaches out beyond the bar. The quarter-notes in the closing "natural scale" are to be taken in the principal tempo, with a hardly perceptible *ritardando* on the final notes.

TO ÉTUDE No. 18

The real difficulty in the celebrated "Study in Thirds" is this; that the player—should not make it seem like a study in thirds. As often the case in Chopin (see the remarks on Nos. 5 and 8), the étude-figure stands out in relief only for brief moments; the "music" lies mostly in the contrasting left-hand parts, which therefore demand special attention. The sultry melancholy of the piece reminds one of a Byronic poem; distinct it must be, and yet appear, as it were, like a gleam from beneath a filmy mourning-veil. The mood of the close is conciliatory, consequently the *Lento* and *f* of the last two measures must be heedfully observed. The fingering here given for the chromatic thirds, first employed by Vladimir de Pachmann (by whom it was probably discovered), can be recommended as the best in view of our present keyboard. The 2d finger slides from the black key down to the first of the two consecutive white keys in both the ascending and descending scales, whereby we most easily approach the *legato*, while rapidity and evenness are wholly unobstructed.

TO ÉTUDE No. 19

Among all Studies in Touch the present one is the most complicated and therefore the most difficult (No. 26 excepted, in a certain sense). The two outer parts perform a duet; between them lies an accompaniment, mostly in two parts, which, barring a few places, progresses in a steady eighth-note rhythm, and should be duly subordinated, whatever the ruling degree of tone-power. Hans von Bülow imagines it as a dialogue between flute and 'cello; not so bad—the 'cello suits admirably; the flute, too, as far as sound goes, but just this instrument, on account of its meagre capacity for modulating and intensifying its tone, is the least adapted of all to serve as a model in this cantilena. So we shall do better to take, as a substitute, the "ideal" wind-instrument suggested in the Note to No. 13. In the course of the seven measures which lead to the close in E♭ major, the entire orchestra really ought to enter gradually. The Introduction, written as a Recitative, should be played almost exactly in time according to the note-values; an excessive *rubato* would be out of keeping with the style of the piece. Play the *ritardando* at the close with great breadth.

TO ÉTUDE No. 20

During practice it will soon be discovered that, in spite of the famous sixths in the right hand, the left-hand part presents the more formidable difficulties; hence, we have to be very particular about this "accompaniment." Among the fingerings for the sixths, which are offered here for his choice, the player will select the one best suited to his hand. The Mikuli fingering in meas. 7, where the thumb is used twelve times in succession, is given here merely as a curiosity; it affords the finest opportunity for stumbling and for needlessly tiring the hand.—All *nuances* are to be "laid on thick." When executed limpidly, this Étude will bear the most rapid tempo.

TO ÉTUDE No. 21

Repeated mention has already been made of the fanciful, arbitrary title. It is seldom suitable, hence usually superfluous, sometimes misleading. Now, in the present case, the name is at least inadequate, and this in the main point. This piece possesses every characteristic of the butterfly; but as regards its fundamental trait, humor, it would be ridiculous to predicate such a thing of butterflies, however many of them might be together. One occasionally hears musicians remark that this Étude is one of the least important of them all; well, it if be taken in a happy-go-lucky, butterfly fashion, the best therein is naturally lost. So view the titles as so many figureheads, whenever the composer himself did not select them.

The thematic figure on which the piece is built up should be carefully examined; the sixteenth-notes, up to the third, are to be played *legato;* the third and fourth, *staccato.* At the *ff,* do not go to an extreme. Do not in any case make a *ritardando* towards the close, otherwise a tinge of sentimentality will creep in which is foreign to the mood; break the Étude off short, sharply, with a flash of wit.

TO ÉTUDE No. 22

The technical aim here is the execution of *legato* octaves. This point would hardly have needed mention, were it not for the fact that some students might at first think that excessive care has been expended on the fingering, precisely in view of the above-noted aim. It is true that a series of octaves may be so bound by skillful pedalling, without changing fingers, as to produce a *legato* effect; but the resulting coloration soon becomes quite different, and that is the point at issue in this piece, apart from its practice as an Étude. Still, wherever a small hand cannot stretch the octave with the third finger, the necessary changes in the fingering can be made without difficulty or material impairment of the total effect, provided that the hand is strong enough for the passages in minor; for in these "storm scenes" the extreme of energy is positively demanded, whereas the lyric portion in **B** major cannot be played too softly and singingly.

TO ÉTUDE No. 23

Chopin's repeatedly mentioned device of employing the given étude-figure as an ornamental trimming for, or commentary on, the musico-thematic content, celebrates its most signal triumph in the present Étude. The left hand has the leading rôle; only once, and but for a moment, does it allow the right hand to take unquestioned thematic precedence. Besides this, the figure in sixteenths bears in its top line a melodic germ which develops further on into a sort of intercessory, tranquillizing counter-motive, though soon lost in silence. But where the figure breaks out in full force, the effect is tremendous. As observed before (see No. 12), this work presents, above all, in its splendid color-scheme the picture of a Revolution with tragic outcome, from the first weirdly muffled call, sounding as in the distance, with its chorale-like echo, to the resonant booming of the passing-bells, and the blood-steeped closing chords.

The secret of endurance to the end, in this Étude, lies in an economical distribution of the strength. However, the more strength one naturally possesses, the better.

TO ÉTUDE No. 24

Here we only need repeat the last lines in the Note to the preceding Étude, concerning economy of strength, applying the remark to both hands. In the *fortissimo* passages one should distinguish between the minor accent > and the stronger ∧. this being an essential point here. Certain sense-twisting misprints, repeated in most of the editions, have been corrected. This piece, too, has recently fallen a victim to the prevalent mania for bestowing titles, now being called the "Ocean Étude." This argues poverty of invention, for ocean-waves do not always run mountain-high. To interpret the close so as to fit the "title," one must picture to himself a successful landing in a great seaport of some country where the Greek-Catholic creed prevails; time, the morning of Christmas or Easter, when the biggest bells are set swinging with a peal that resounds for miles.

TO ÉTUDE No. 25

In this Étude we are once more confronted with a poem—a Night Vision. Broodingly it takes its course in sullen *Weltschmerz*, in wrath repressed and lofty disdain, scarce cheered by a ray of light—then suddenly fades resignedly away. When Liszt played it, he usually went back from the 11th measure before the end to the corresponding place in the 22nd measure from the beginning, and repeated this entire part, bringing out the contours still more sharply and incisively.

TO ÉTUDE No. 26

Another Étude which is a poem—now of an essentially different content. Here reign deep repose and blessed peace. The shadows swiftly flitting by should be conceived only as painless, transfigured memories of sorrows long since vanquished; for these tones are borne to us out of a world where all strife ceases and all differences are healed. In its inmost spirit this piece ranks high above No. 19; for the latter, with all its beauty, is still wholly "of this world." Thus we now find it harder to obtain an adequate effect. Beware, first of all, of over-hastening the tempo in the slightest; observe a strict *legato*, with and without pedal, always treat the incidental contrasting parts with quietly expressive effect, and take the single *f* and the *più f* immediately following as heavy, sustained accents.

Liszt was very fond of playing this Étude. Indeed, it was the last piece that his friends heard him play, and none then present can ever forget it. It is this impression which the above observations seek to convey.

TO ÉTUDE No. 27

Had Chopin chosen the title "Trois Poésies" instead of "Trois Études," many a thoughtful pianist would have been peculiarly grateful to him just in this case; but such a thing was repugnant to him. However, this is, in any event, an Étude, viewed from a purely technical standpoint, since merely a thoroughly correct execution, with precise observance of the marks of interpretation, is far harder than appears at first sight. As to mood, this piece holds nearly a middle course between the pessimism of No. 25 and the transfiguration of No. 26. Here everything is so soulfully-thoughtfully serene, flowing onward easily and gracefully. Although vacillating in tempo between Mazurka and slow Waltz, an actual dance-rhythm must never be brought to the fore; that is not wanted here.

ÉTUDES

THE ÉTUDES

I

THE Études of Chopin are not only the foundation of his technical system—a system new to pianism when they appeared—but they also comprise some of his most imaginative and enchanting creations, judged exclusively from the musical point of view. Therefore it behooves us to make a somewhat extended investigation of their origins, though for obvious reasons not a comparative critical estimate of various editions. I say "for obvious reasons" because this present edition is definitive and, while adhering to the purity of the original Chopin text, avoids the numerous errors of preceding editions. Suffice it to say that the first complete edition of the Chopin works was Gebethner & Wolff's, of Warsaw; Karasowski gives the date of publication as 1846. Since then, the deluge: Tellefsen, Klindworth, Scholtz, Mikuli, Kahnt, Schuberth, Steingräber—Mertke—Schlesinger (edited by Theodor Kullak), Reinecke, Xaver Scharwenka, von Bülow, D.. Hugo Riemann—the Études and a few of the Preludes—and Hermann Scholtz. Fontana, Wolff, Gutmann, Mikuli, Tellefsen, Mathias, pupils of Chopin, copied from the original manuscripts, and yet they cannot agree, not only as to phrasing and various *tempi*, but even as to integrity of the text. The errors of certain editions are notorious, nor have modern editions mended matters. By universal assent Mikuli's edition has been pronounced the least defective; yet it leaves much to be desired. In following the Études I shall avoid too many comparisons, for in that case the student would not be able to see the forest because of the trees; above all, no mention of metronome marks, as the action of the modern pianoforte greatly differs from the Pleyel of Chopin's days; the *tempi* then would be old-fashioned now.

Frédéric Chopin, aged twenty, wrote in Warsaw on October 20, 1829, to his friend, Titus Woyciechowski: "I have composed a Study in my own manner"; and in November 14th the same year: "I have written some Studies; in your presence I should play them well." Thus quite modestly did the Polish composer announce an event that proved to be of supreme importance to the piano-playing world. Niecks thinks these Studies were published in the Summer of 1833, July or August, and were numbered opus 10. Another set of Studies, opus 25, did not find a publisher till 1837, though a number of them were composed at the same time as the previous work. A Polish musician who visited the French capital in 1834 heard Chopin play the Studies contained in opus 25. The C minor Study, opus 10, No. 12, commonly known as the "Revolutionary," was born at Stuttgart, September, 1831,"while under the excitement caused by the news of the taking of Warsaw by the Russians, on September 8th, 1831." These dates are given so as to dispel the suspicion that Liszt had influenced Chopin in the production of these masterpieces. In her exhaustive biography of Liszt, Lina Ramann declares that Nos. 9 and 12 of opus 10, and Nos. 11 and 12 of opus 25, reveal the influence of the Hungarian virtuoso. But figures prove the fallacy of her assertion. The influence was in the other direction, as Liszt's three Concert Studies show—not to mention other of his compositions. When Chopin arrived at Paris his style was formed, he was the creator of a new piano technique. The Studies, known as Trois Nouvelles Études, which appeared in 1840 in the Moscheles and Fétis Method of Methods, were afterward separately published. We do not know their date of composition. The manuscript was given to the Princess M. Czartoryska by the composer's sister after his death. The Chopin Studies are poems fit for Parnassus, yet they also serve a very useful purpose in pedagogy. The poetry and passion of the Ballades and Scherzi wind throughout these technical problems like a flaming skein. Both aspects, the material and spiritual, should not be overlooked.

In the first Study of the first book, opus 10, dedicated to Liszt, Chopin at a leap reached new land. Extended chords had been sparingly used by Hummel and Clementi, but to take a dispersed harmony and transform it into an epical Study, to raise the chord of the tenth to heroic stature—only Chopin could have accomplished such a miracle. This first Study in C Major is veritably heroic. The irregular black ascending and descending staircases of notes give the neophyte giddiness. Like the marvellous architectural dreams of Piranesi, these dizzy acclivities and descents of Chopin exercise a hypnotic charm on eye as well as ear. Here in all its nakedness is the new technique: new in the sense of figure, pattern, web, new in a harmonic way. The old order was horrified at the modulatory harshness, the younger generation fascinated and also a trifle frightened. A man who could thus explode a mine that assailed the stars must be reckoned with. The nub of modern piano music is in this study, the most formally reckless ever penned by Chopin. Von Bülow rightfully inveighed against the pervading disposition to play the octave basses arpeggiated; in fact these basses are the argument of the play; they should be granitic, ponderable, powerful. This Study suggests that its composer wished to begin the exposition of his technical system with a skeletonized statement. It is the tree stripped of its bark, the flower of its leaves, yet austere as is the result there are compensating dignity, unswerving logic. With this Study he unlocked, not his heart, but the kingdom of technique. It might for variety's sake be played in unison.

Von Bülow writes that as the second Study in A minor is chromatically related to the Moscheles Étude, opus 70, No. 3, that piece could be used to pave the way for the more musical composition of the Pole. In different degrees of *tempi*, dynamics and rhythmic accent it should be practised, omitting the thumb and first finger. The entire composition, with its murmuring, meandering, chromatic character, is a forerunner to the whispering, weaving, moonlit effects in some of the later Studies. In the third Study we get the intimate Chopin. Its key is E major and it is among the finest flowering of his garden; it is simpler, less morbid, sultry and languorous than the much praised Study in C sharp minor, opus 25, No. 7. Niecks thinks that this Study "may be counted among Chopin's loveliest compositions . . . it combines classical chasteness of contour with the fragrance of romanticism." Chopin told his faithful pupil, Gutmann, that "he had never in his life written another such melody," and once when hearing it played he raised his arms and cried out: "O ma patrie!"

How well Chopin knew the value of contrast in sentiment and tonality may be observed in the next Study, No. 4. A classic is this piece, which, despite its dark key-color, C sharp minor, as a foil to the preceding one in E, bubbles with life and fairly spurts flame. It recalls the story of the Polish peasantry who are happiest when they sing in the minor mode. The technics of this composition do not lie beneath the surface; they are very much in the way of clumsy fingers and heavy wrists. We wonder why this Study does not figure more frequently in piano recitals. It is a healthy technical test, it is brilliant, and the *coda* is dramatic. Ten bars before the return of the theme there is a stiff digital hedge to jump. The so-called "Black Key" Study No. 5 is familiar and a favorite. It is full of Polish elegance. Von Bülow rather disdainfully speaks of it as a Salon Étude. It is certainly graceful, delicately witty, a trifle naughty, arch, roguish, and delightfully invented. Technically it requires velvet-tipped fingers and a supple wrist. A dark, doleful nocturne is the Study No. 6, in E flat minor. Its melody is full of stifled sorrow. The figure is ingenious and subordinated to the theme. In the E major section the music broadens to dramatic vigor. Chopin was not quite the slave of

his mood. There must be a psychical programme to this Study, some record of a youthful disillusion, but its expression is kept well within continent lines. The Sarmatian composer has not yet unlearned the value of reserve. We emerge into a clearer, a more bracing atmosphere in the C major Study, No. 7. It is a genuine toccata, with moments of tender twilight, withal serving a distinct technical purpose—the study of double-notes changing on one key—and is as sane as the Toccata by Schumann. Here is a brave, an undaunted Chopin, a gay cavalier with the sunshine shimmering about him. There are times when this Study seems like light peeping through the trees in a mysterious forest. With the *delicato* there are Puck-like rustlings, and all the while the pianist is exercising wrists and fingers with a technical exercise. Were ever Beauty and Duty mated so in double-harness? Pegasus pulling a rain-charged cloud over arid land. For study purposes the playing of the entire composition with wrist stroke is advisable; it will secure clear articulation, staccato and finger-memory, also compass more quickly the elusive, flitting character of the piece.

How the F major Study, No. 8, makes the piano sound. What a rich, brilliant sweep it achieves. It elbows the treble to its last euphonious point, glitters and crests itself, only to fall away as if the sea were melodic and could shatter and tumble into tuneful foam. The emotional content is not remarkable, the composition is for the salon or concert hall. At its close one catches the overtones of bustling plaudits and the clapping of gloved palms. Ductility, an aristocratic ease, a delicate touch and fluent technique will carry off this Study with good effect. Technically it is useful—one must speak of the usefulness of Chopin even in these imprisoned irridescent bubbles. A slower *tempo* than the old marking is not amiss, as the Herz and Czerny ideal of velocity vanished with the shallow dip of the keys in Chopin's days—which had much to do with the swiftness and lightness of his playing. The nobler, more sonorous tone of the latter-day concert grand demands greater breadth of style, less speedy passage-work. There can be no doubt as to the wisdom of a broader treatment of this charming display piece. The F minor Study, No. 9, is the first one of his tone studies in which the mood is more petulant than tempestuous. This melody is morbid, almost irritatingly so, and yet not without a certain accent of grandeur. There is a persistency of repetition that foreshadows the Chopin of the later, sadder years. The figure in the left hand is the first in which a prominent part is given that member. Not as noble and sonorous a figure as the one in the C minor Study, it may be viewed as a distinct forerunner to the bass of the D minor Prelude, opus 28, No. 24. The stretch in the F minor Study is the technical object. It is rather awkward for close-knit fingers.

The next Study in A flat, No. 10, is one of the most charming in the series. There is more depth in it than in the G flat and F major Studies, and its effectiveness on the virtuoso side is unquestionable. A savor of the salon is in its perfumed measures, but there are grace, spontaneity and happiness. Chopin must have been as happy as his sensitive nature permitted him when he conceived this vivacious caprice. A musical Corot, if such a comparison be allowed, is the Study No. 11. Its novel design, delicate arabesques—as if the guitar had been dowered with a soul—and the richness and originality of its harmonic scheme, give us pause to ask if Chopin's technical invention is not almost boundless. The harmonization, with the dispersed position of the underlying harmonies, is far more wonderful; but nowadays the chord of the tenth and more remote intervals seem no longer daring; modern composition has devilled the musical alphabet into the caverns of the grotesque; nevertheless, there are harmonies on the last page of this Study that still excite wonder. The fifteenth bar from the end is one that Richard Wagner must have admired, and from that bar to the close every group is masterly. Remember, this Study is a nocturne. It should not be taken at too speedy a *tempo*. The color-scheme is celestial, the ending a sigh, not unmixed with happiness. Chopin had his moments of content. The dizzy *appoggiatura* leaps in the last few bars set the seal of perfection upon this unique composition. Few pianists produce the aerial effect, the swaying of the tone-tendrils abounding in the composition. Yet this exquisite flight into the blue, this nocturne which should be played before sundown, excited the astonishment of Mendelssohn, the perplexity and wrath of Moscheles, and the contempt of Rellstab,

editor of the "Iris," who wrote in that journal in 1834 about the Studies opus 10: "Those who have distorted fingers may put them right by practising these Studies; but those who have not, should not play them, at least, not without a surgeon at hand."

We have now arrived at the last Study in opus 10, the magnificent one in C minor, No. 12. In it the young Polish eagle begins to face the sun, begins to mount on wind-weaving pinions. Four pages suffice for a background upon which the composer has flung with overwhelming fury the darkest, the most demoniacal expressions of his nature. Here no veiled surmise, no smothered rage, but all sweeps along in tornadic passion. Karasowski's story may be true or not regarding the genesis of the work; but true or not, it is one of the greatest dramatic outbursts in the literature of the piano. Powerful in design, pride, force and speed, it never relaxes its grim grip from the first shrill dissonance to the overwhelming chordal close. The end rings out like the crack of creation. It is elemental. Karasowski writes: "Grief, anxiety, despair over the fate of his relations and his dearly beloved father filled the measures of his sufferings." (The fall of Warsaw into the hands of the Russians, alluded to above.) "Under the influence of this mood he wrote the C minor Étude, called the Revolutionary. Out of the mad and tempestuous storm of passages for the left hand the melody arises aloft, now passionate and anon proudly majestic, until thrills of awe stream over the listener, and the image is evoked of Zeus hurling thunderbolts at the world." The Study is full of pathos; it compasses the sublime, and yet in its most torrential moments the composer never loses his intellectual equipoise. It has but one rival in the Chopin Studies—No. 12, opus 25, in the same key.

II

Twelve Studies, opus 25, are dedicated to the Countess d'Agoult, the mother of Liszt's children. The set opens with the familiar study in A flat, so familiar that I shall not make much ado about it except to say that it is delicious, but played often and badly. For Schumann it was an Æolian harp "possessed of all the musical scales." All that modern editing has accomplished for it is to hunt up fresh accentuations, so that the piece is become almost a study in false accents. Chopin, as Schumann has pointed out, did not permit every one of the small notes to be distinctly heard. "It was rather an undulation of the A flat major chord, here and there thrown aloft by the pedal." The twenty-fourth bar is so Lisztian that Liszt must have benefitted by its harmonies.

"And then he played the second in the book, in F minor, one in which his individuality displays itself in a manner never to be forgotten. How charming, how dreamy it was! Soft as the song of

a sleeping child." Schumann wrote this about the study in F minor, opus 25, No. 2, which whispers not of baleful deeds in a dream, as does the last movement of the B flat minor Sonata, but is indeed "the song of a sleeping child." No comparison can be prettier, for there is a sweet, delicate drone that sometimes issues from childish lips possessing a charm for ears attuned to poetry. This must have been the Study that Chopin played for Henrietta Voigt at Leipsic, September 12, 1836. She said: "The over-excitement of his fantastic manner is imparted to the keen-eared. It made me hold my breath. Wonderful is the ease with which his velvet fingers glide, I might say fly, over the keys. He has enraptured me—in a way which hitherto had been unknown to me. What delighted me was the childlike, natural manner which he showed in his demeanor and in his playing." Von Bülow believes that the interpretation of the magical music should be without sentimentality, almost without shading

—clearly, delicately and dreamily executed. "An ideal *pianissimo*, an accentless quality, and completely without passion or *rubato*." There is little doubt that this was the way Chopin played it. Liszt is an authority on the subject and Georges Mathias corroborates him. It should be played in that Chopin whisper of which Mendelssohn said "that for him nothing more enchanting existed." This Study contains much beauty, and every bar rules over a little harmonic kingdom. It is so lovely that not even the Brahms distortion in double-notes can dull its magnetic crooning. At times its design is so delicate that it recalls the faint, fantastic traceries made by frost on glass. As a Study in mixed rhythms it is valuable. Rubinstein and Annette Essipowa ended it with echo-like effects on the four C's, the pedal floating the tone. Schumann thinks the third study in F major less novel in character, although "here the master showed his admirable bravura powers." It is a spirited caprice with four different voices, if one pulls apart the brightly colored petals of the thematic flower, and thus reveals the chemistry of its delicate growth. "The third voice is the chief one, and after it the first, because they determine the melodic and harmonic contents," writes Kullak. The profile of the melody is in the eighth-notes. They give the meaning to the decorative pattern. And what charm, buoyancy and sweetness there are in this caprice. It has the elusive, tantalizing charm of a hummingbird in flight. The human element is almost eliminated. We are in the open. The sun blazes in the blue. Even when the tone deepens, when the shadows grow cooler and darker in the B major section, there is little hint of sadness. The harmonic shifts are subtle, admirable, the everchanging devices of the figuration. The fourth study in A minor is a rather sombre, nervous composition, which besides being an Étude also indicates a slightly pathologic condition. With its breath-catching syncopations and narrow emotional range it has its moments of interest if not actual power. Stephen Heller said that this study reminded him of the first bar of the Kyrie—rather the Requiem Æternam of Mozart's Requiem. If not taken at a rapid pace the *cantilena* is heard to better advantage.

It is safe to say that the fifth study in E minor is less often heard in the concert room than any of its companions. Yet it is a sonorous piano piece, rich in embroideries and decorative effect in the middle section. Perhaps the rather perverse, capricious and not too amiable character of the opening page has made pianists wary of playing it in recital. The middle part, with its melody for the thumb and arpeggios, recalls Thalberg. It was Louis Ehlert who wrote of the Study in G sharp minor, No. 6, "Chopin not only versifies an exercise in thirds; he transforms it into such a work of art that in studying it one could sooner fancy himself on Parnassus than at a lesson." And in all piano literature there is no more remarkable example of the merging of matter and manner. The means justifies the end, and the means employed by the composer in this instance are beautiful; beautiful is the word that best describes the architectonics of this study. With the Schumann Toccata, the G sharp minor study stands at the portals of the delectable land of Double-Notes. Both compositions have a common ancestry in the Czerny Toccata. After reading through all the double-note studies for the instrument it is in the nature of a miracle to come upon Chopin's transfiguration of such a barren and mechanical exercise. His study is first music, then a technical problem. Here is not the place to discuss the different fingerings. Each virtuoso has his predilection. What fingering Chopin preferred is aside from the mark, for the action of his piano was easy compared with ours. Von Bülow calls the seventh study in C sharp minor a nocturne, a duo for 'cello and flute. Its dialogue is intimate in feeling. For the contemporaries of Chopin it was one of his greatest efforts. In it are traces of life-weariness. It is both morbid and elegiac. There is nostalgia in its measures, the nostalgia of a sick soul. The D flat Study, No. 8, has been described as the most useful exercise in the whole range of Étude literature. It is an admirable study in double-sixths and is euphonious, even in the passage of consecutive fifths that formerly set theorists at odds. The nimble study that follows, in the key of G flat, No. 9, usually bears the title of "The Butterfly." It is graceful rather than deep and is a prime favorite as an encore piece. It has been compared to a Charles Mayer composition, but the boot is on the other leg. Asiatic in its wildness is the B minor study, No. 10. Its monophonic character recalls the Chorus of Dervishes in Beethoven's "Ruins of Athens." Niecks finds it "a real pandemonium." This Étude is technically an important one. The opening, portentous and sour, becomes a driving whirlwind of tone. There is lushness in the octave melody; the tune may be a little overripe, but it is sweet, sensuous music and about it hovers the hush of a rich evening in early autumn. The close is dramatic.

The canvas of the A minor study, the "Winter Wind," No. 11, is Chopin's largest—thus far—in this opus 25. Not even in the two Concertos is there the resistless overflow of this Étude, which has been justly compared to the screaming of wintry blasts. The theme is never relaxed and its fluctuating harmonic surprises are many. The end is notable for the fact that scales appear: Chopin seldom uses scale-figures in his Studies (and trills sparingly). From Hummel to Herz and Thalberg the keyboard had glittered with spangled scales. Chopin must have been sick of them, as sick as he was of the left-hand melody with arpeggiated figures in the right *à la* Thalberg. In the first C sharp minor Study, opus 10, there is a run for the left hand in the *coda*. In the seventh Study, similar key, opus 25, there are more. The second Study, in A minor, opus 10, is a chromatic scale study; but there are no other specimens in this form till the mighty run at the conclusion of the A minor Study, opus 25, No. 11. Of course, this doesn't apply to the A flat Polonaise, opus 53, or other compositions. The Study in question demands power and endurance. Also passion and no little poetry. It is true storm-music, and the theme in the bass moves throughout in processional splendor. The prime technical difficulty is the management of the thumb, but the didactic side need not concern us here. As for the last Study in opus 25, the C minor, No. 12, I may only add that it is something more than an "exercise in unbroken chord passages for both hands," as has been said. It is grandiose, and there is a primeval, naked simplicity in its tumultuous measures that reveals the puissant soul of Chopin. And it is eloquent. It is rugged. An epic of the piano, it is far removed from the musical dandyism of the drawing-room. Chopin here is Chopin the Conqueror.

III

In 1840, "Trois nouvelles Études" by Frédéric Chopin appeared in the "Méthode des Méthodes pour le piano par I. Moscheles et F. J. Fétis." Odd company for the Polish composer. "Internal evidence seems to show," says Niecks, "that these weakest of the master's Studies—which, however, are by no means uninteresting and certainly very characteristic—may be regarded, more than opus 25, as the outcome of a gleaning." But the last two decades have contributed much to the artistic stature of these three supplementary Studies (which are sometimes erroneously described as posthumous, though published nine years before the composer's death). They have something of the concision of the Preludes. The first is admirable. In F minor, the theme in triplet quarters, broad, sonorous, passionate, is unequally pitted against eighth-notes in the bass. A rhythmic problem, this, and not difficult to solve. It is the emotional content that attracts. Deeper than the F minor Study in opus 25 is this one, and though the doors never swing wide open we may divine the tragic issues concealed. Beautiful in a different way is the A flat Study that follows; again the problem is a rhythmic one, and again the composer demonstrates his seemingly exhaustless invention, and his power in evoking a single mood, envisaging its lovely contours and letting it melt away as if dream-magic. Replete with gentle sprightliness and lingering sweetness is this Study. Chopin, like Wagner, possesses a hypnotic mastery over his auditors. Don't bother your head over the "triplicity in biplicity" of Kullak, or the pedantry of von Bülow—whose brain was surely compart-mentized like an apothecary's shelves. Too many editors spoil the music. In all the editions save one that I have seen, the third Study in D flat begins on A flat, like the popular waltz in D flat. The exception is Klindworth, who starts with B flat, the note above. This Study is flooded with sunny good-humor and arouses the most cheering thoughts. Its technical aim is a simultaneous performance of *legato* and *staccato*. The result is like an idealized Waltz in *allegretto* movement, the incarnation of joy tempered by aristocratic reserve. Chopin never romps, but he jests wittily and always with taste. This Study fitly closes his remarkable labors in the form, and it is as if he had signed it—"F. Chopin *et ego in Arcady.*"

Our admiration for the Studies is tinged with wonder at such a prodigal display of thematic and technical invention. Their variety is great, the æsthetic side is never neglected for the mechanical, and in the most poetic of them stuff may be found for delicate as well as heroic fingers. These Studies are exemplary essays in style and emotion. In them all Chopin is mirrored. When most of his piano music has gone the way of things fashioned by mortal hands, these Studies will still endure; will stand for the nineteenth century, as Beethoven crystallized the eighteenth, Bach the seventeenth centuries, in the music of the pianoforte. Chopin is a classic.

James Hüneker

Thematic Index

À F. Liszt

Douze grandes Études

Revised and fingered by
Arthur Friedheim

F. CHOPIN. Op. 10, No. 1

Allegro (♩ = 144)

1.

Copyright, 1916, by G. Schirmer, Inc.

Revised and fingered by
Arthur Friedheim

Étude

F. CHOPIN. Op. 10, No. 2

Allegro ($\bullet$ = 126)

2.

Étude

Revised and fingered by
Arthur Friedheim

F. CHOPIN. Op. 10, No. 3

Lento ma non troppo (♪ = 69)

3.

Étude

F. CHOPIN. Op. 10, No. 4

Revised and fingered by
Arthur Friedheim

Étude

Vivace (♩ = 116)
Brillante

F. CHOPIN. Op.10, No.5

Copyright, 1916, by G. Schirmer, Inc.
Printed in the U.S.A.

Étude

Revised and fingered by
Arthur Friedheim

F. CHOPIN. Op. 10, No. 6

Revised and fingered by
Arthur Friedheim

Douze grandes Études

F. CHOPIN. Op. 10, No. 7

Vivace

7.

Revised and fingered by
Arthur Friedheim

Étude

F. CHOPIN. Op. 10, No. 8

Allegro (♩ = 88)

8.

veloce e sempre legato

Étude

Revised and fingered by
Arthur Friedheim

F. CHOPIN. Op. 10, No. 9

Printed in the U.S.A.
Copyright, 1916, by G. Schirmer, Inc.

Étude

Revised and fingered by
Arthur Friedheim

F. CHOPIN. Op. 10, No. 10

Vivace assai (♩. = 92)

10.

Étude

Revised and fingered by
Arthur Friedheim

F. CHOPIN. Op. 10, No. 11

11.

Allegretto (♩ = 72)

Revised and fingered by
Arthur Friedheim

Étude

F. CHOPIN. Op. 10, No. 12

Allegro con fuoco ($\quad = 144$)

12.

à Mme la Comtesse d'Agoult

Douze Études

Revised and fingered by
Arthur Friedheim

F. CHOPIN. Op. 25, No. 1

Allegro sostenuto (♩ = 84)

13.

Revised and fingered by
Arthur Friedheim

Étude

F. CHOPIN. Op. 25, No. 2

Presto (♩ = 112)

14.

p
molto legato

Étude

Revised and fingered by
Arthur Friedheim

F. CHOPIN. Op. 25, No. 3

15.

Allegro (♩ = 120)

leggiero.

p

poco marcato

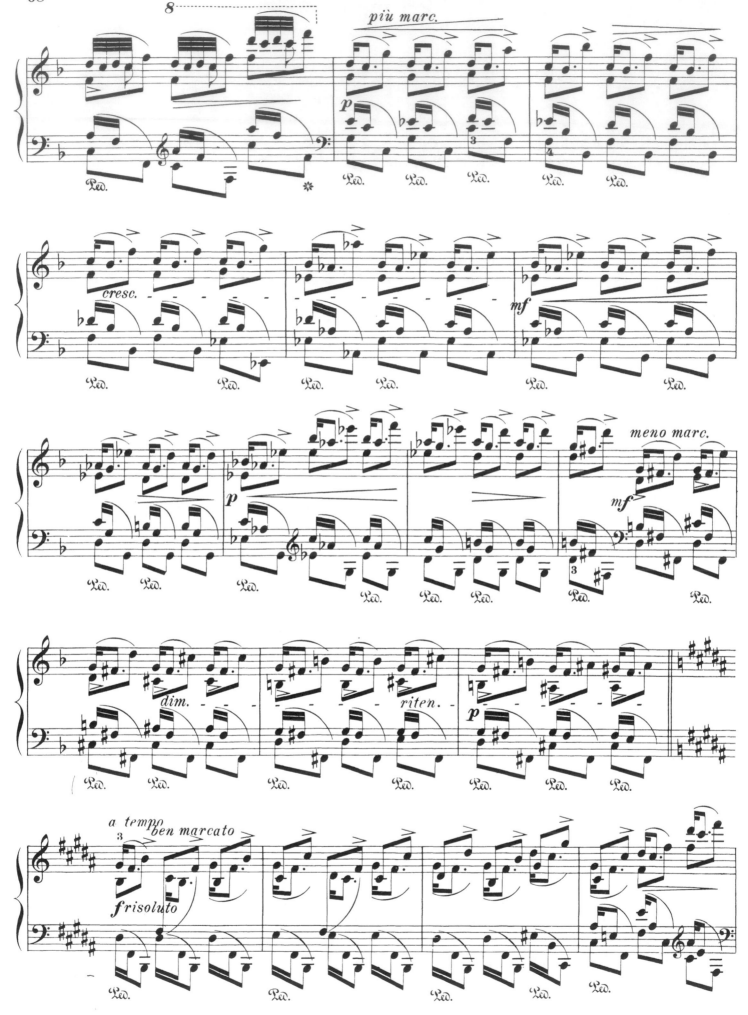

Étude

Revised and fingered by
Arthur Friedheim

F. CHOPIN. Op. 25, No. 4

Agitato (♩=160)

16.

Revised and fingered by
Arthur Friedheim

Étude

F. CHOPIN. Op. 25, No. 5

17.

Revised and fingered by
Arthur Friedheim

Étude

F. CHOPIN. Op. 25, No. 6

Allegro (♩= 69)

18.

sotto voce

Copyright, 1916, by G. Schirmer, Inc.

Étude

Revised and fingered by
Arthur Friedheim

F. CHOPIN. Op. 25, No. 7

19.

Revised and fingered by
Arthur Friedheim

Étude

F. CHOPIN. Op. 25, No. 8

Vivace legato (♩ = 80)

20.

Revised and fingered by
Arthur Friedheim

Étude

Allegro vivace (♩= 112)

F. CHOPIN. Op. 25, No. 9

21.

Revised and fingered by
Arthur Friedheim

Étude

F. CHOPIN. Op. 25, No. 10

Allegro con fuoco (♩ = 60)

22.

Étude

Revised and fingered by
Arthur Friedheim

F. CHOPIN. Op. 25, No. 11

23.

Étude

110 Revised and fingered by Arthur Friedheim

Allegro molto, con fuoco ($\quarternote = 76$)

F. CHOPIN. Op. 25. No. 12

24.

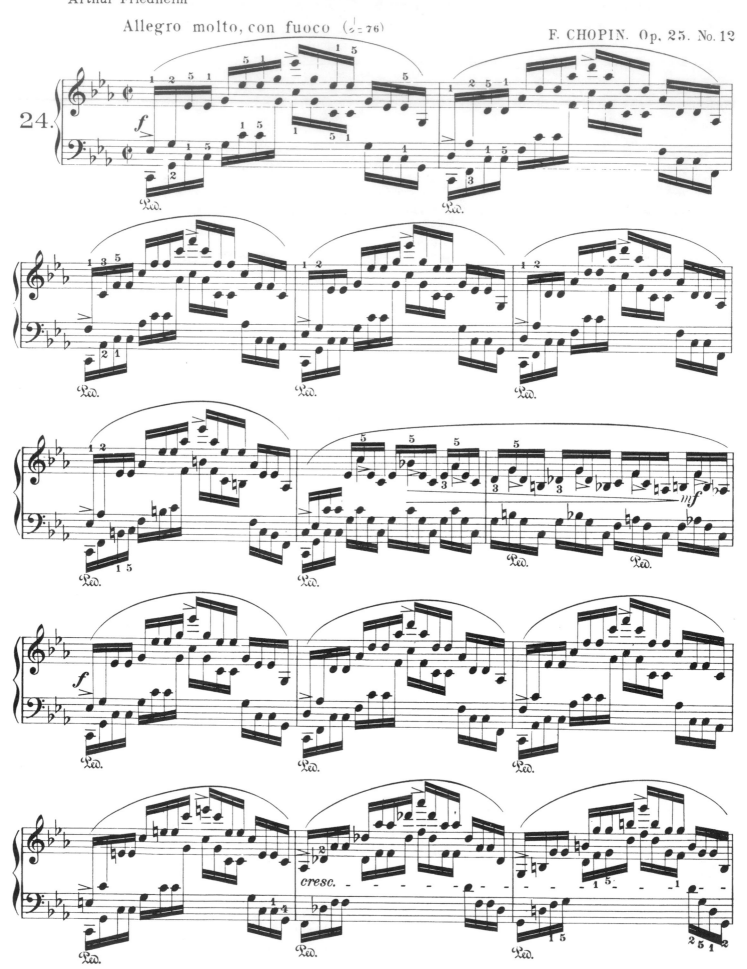

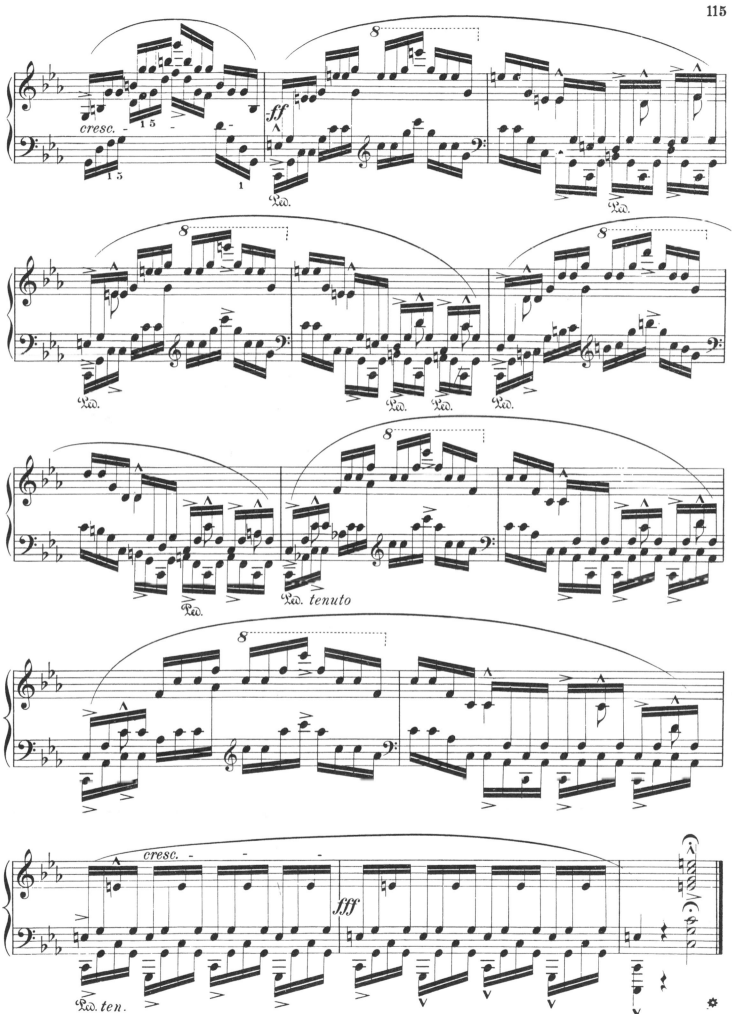

Trois Études

Revised and fingered by
Arthur Friedheim

(Composées pour la Méthode de Moscheles et Fétis)

Nº 1

Andantino (♩ = 120)

F. CHOPIN

Trois Études

Revised and fingered by
Arthur Friedheim

(Composeés pour la Méthode de Moscheles et Fétis)

F. CHOPIN

Nº 2

Allegretto (♩=58)

26.

Trois Études

Revised and fingered by
Arthur Friedheim

(Composées pour la Méthode de Moscheles et Fétis)

No. 3 *legato*

F. CHOPIN

Allegretto (♩=168)

27.